Other books by Rachel Saunders

The Blue Chair Jam Cookbook
Blue Chair Cooks with Jam & Marmalade

I LOVE JAM

RACHEL SAUNDERS

Photography by Sara Remington

**Andrews McMeel
Publishing®**

a division of Andrews McMeel Universal

CONTENTS

INTRODUCTION

Making jam and marmalade can be more than a hobby—it can be a life passion, and a wonderful way to connect with your surroundings. Capturing the vivid flavor of local fruit in jars is addictive. Throughout these pages, you will find delicious jam recipes for all your favorite fruits, plus several mouthwatering ideas for how to cook and bake with your creations. I have also included many tips and ideas for recipe variations, providing you with the tools you need to create your own special jams and marmalades.

Enjoy!

WHAT IS THE DIFFERENCE BETWEEN JAM, JELLY & MARMALADE?

A jam is a spreadable fruit preserve consisting of pieces of fruit cooked with sugar until they thicken and partially break down.

A jelly is a clear preserve made from cooked fruit juice that has been combined with sugar, lemon juice, and (sometimes) added pectin and boiled until it sets.

A marmalade (shown at left) is a jelly with clearly defined pieces of fruit (usually citrus) suspended in it.

A fruit butter is a sweetened fruit purée cooked until it reaches a concentrated, smooth, spreadable, paste-like consistency.

A fruit cheese or paste is a high-pectin fruit butter cooked until it has thickened and lost enough moisture to form a solid, sliceable mass when cool.

SUGAR, ACID & PECTIN: THE THREE BUILDING BLOCKS FOR PRESERVING

All preserves require a perfect balance of sugar, acid, and pectin. Each plays a different and essential role in the preserving process:

SUGAR sweetens, preserves, and thickens the cooked fruit. All preserves require some form of sugar. White cane sugar is best; it gives preserves a superb texture and shows off the natural flavor of the fruit.

ACID sharpens the fruit's flavor and helps give the jam its proper texture. Lemon juice, the most useful acid, brightens and balances the preserve's flavor. Citric and ascorbic acids, both naturally derived, help prolong the preserve's shelf life and add extra bite.

PECTIN is a complex carbohydrate molecule found in all fruits to a varying degree. When fruit is heated, its natural pectin is released. As the cooking progresses, moisture evaporates and the molecules of pectin get closer together, eventually reaching a perfect "setting" point at which they can lock with each other. This enables the jam to thicken to a spreadable consistency as it cools. Because nearly all fruits naturally have enough pectin for the jam to reach the desired texture, adding extra pectin is almost never necessary.

THE JAM PAN

You will need a very large, wide pan to make a very small batch. This is essential, as it allows a maximum of evaporation to occur in a minimum of time. A copper jam pan is ideal, but enameled cast iron and stainless steel will also work. Never use unlined aluminum for preserving.

Your raw ingredients should be a few inches deep at the outset of the final cooking. If you are using a smaller pan than suggested, adjust the quantity of raw ingredients accordingly; keep the ideal depth of fruit in mind, since you may need to cook the preserve in two or more small batches instead of one big one.

THE FOUR STAGES OF COOKING A JAM OR MARMALADE

Initial Heating: The mixture heats up gradually, dissolving any undissolved sugar.

Initial Bubbling and Foaming: Once hot, the mixture starts bubbling and/or foaming and the raw fruit pieces release all of their moisture into the mixture.

Final Bubbling and Foaming: As the volume of the mixture goes down and its moisture content decreases, the mixture becomes denser, more concentrated, and darker in color. You may need to lower the heat slightly at this point to prevent burning.

Final Phase: In order to eliminate the final bits of excess moisture and achieve a perfect texture, the jam is cooked for just a few extra minutes at the tail end of the process.

HOW TO KNOW WHEN YOUR JAM IS FINISHED COOKING

When testing for doneness, remember that preserves often thicken significantly as they cool to room temperature.

Since only preserves with an extremely high sugar ratio will reach the 220°F setting point, it is important to know what to actually look for to tell whether a preserve is done. A combination of the freezer test and a visual examination of the preserve works best:

This raspberry jam is sheeting off the spoon, indicating doneness.

The crinkly skin on this marmalade indicates that it is ready.

SIGNS & TESTS OF DONENESS

Bubbles and Foam: A preserve's bubbles change as it cooks, typically becoming either larger and more sputtering (low-sugar jams and fruit butters) or tiny and shiny (most jellies, marmalades, and high-sugar jams).

Appearance: A finished preserve has a slight shine to it, because its concentration of sugar has increased so much during the cooking process. The fruit often becomes suspended in the mixture, rather than floating to the top or sinking to the bottom; this can indicate that the proper balance of moisture, acid, and pectin has been reached.

Ability to Sheet: Dip a metal spoon in the preserve and hold the spoon perpendicular to the pot at a slight vertical angle while the preserve drips back into the pan. If the preserve is done, the drips will tend to run along the bottom edge of the spoon to collect into one big drip (this is known as sheeting). The final drips may tend to cling to the spoon and form little pearl-like drops.

The jam from this freezer test runs easily off the spoon, indicating the jam still needs to cook a few more minutes.

After a few more minutes of cooking, the jam is thickened and no longer runs off the spoon.

Ability to Form a Skin: Let the preserve sit in the pot undisturbed for a few minutes off the heat. If, after a few minutes, the preserve has thickened slightly and started forming a skin across the top, it is likely done. If, however, little liquidy areas have formed on the surface and there is no clear skin forming, it is probably not quite ready yet.

The Freezer Test: Place five metal spoons on a saucer in the freezer before you start cooking the preserve. When you think the preserve might be ready, remove it from the heat, scoop a representative half-spoonful (one containing both the liquidy and the more solid portions), and carefully transfer it onto one of the frozen spoons. Put the cold spoon back in the freezer for three to four minutes. Then, remove the spoon from the freezer and carefully feel the underside. It should be neither warm nor cold; if still warm, return it to the freezer for a moment. Tilt the spoon vertically to see if the preserve runs; depending on the individual preserve, it should run either slowly (jams) or not at all. If it has not yet reached the appropriate point, return the pot to the stove, cook it for another three to four minutes, and test again.

STERILIZATION & STORAGE

When making preserves, be sure to sterilize your jars and lids, unless you plan to eat your jam right away. There are many ways to sterilize jars, including putting them in a canning kettle or a sterilizing dishwasher, but my preferred way is in the oven. This method is easier than the other methods and, if you use an oven thermometer, is virtually foolproof.

HOW TO STERILIZE YOUR JARS USING THE OVEN METHOD

First, be sure your jars are perfectly clean.

Place the clean jars upright with an equal number of clean, unused lids on a baking sheet or sheet pan in a pre-heated 250°F oven. They should remain in the oven for a minimum of thirty minutes to ensure that they are heated through.

When you are ready to fill your jars, remove them from the oven, keeping the oven at 250°F.

Fill your jars, leaving ¼ inch of room at the top.

Before lidding each jar, wipe its rim with a clean, damp cloth.

Lid the filled jars, being careful to screw the lids on just until they are snug.

Replace the filled jars in the oven for fifteen minutes or so to ensure that they are completely sterilized.

Remove the jars from the oven and place them 1 inch apart on a drying rack to set overnight at room temperature. Do not jiggle or disturb them during this time, as this may disrupt their ability to set correctly.

Before putting your preserves away, be sure to feel the top of each lid to verify that it has sealed; it should be curving in very slightly in the middle. If any jars have not sealed, put them in the refrigerator for safekeeping.

To store sealed preserves, label and date them and keep them in a cool, dark place until you open them. After you open a jar, keep it in the refrigerator. You may also keep high-sugar preserves at room temperature, assuming you plan to eat them within a few weeks or so. Low-sugar preserves should always be refrigerated once opened, unless you plan to consume them right away.

Sometimes, the jars can become a little bit too hot when using the oven-sterilization method, so before filling them, test their temperature first. Pour a little jam into one, and if it bubbles or boils in the jar, wait a few moments before filling the jars.

RECIPES

Once you have made your jam, there are many delicious things you can make—so much so, in fact, that I devoted an entire book, *Blue Chair Cooks with Jam & Marmalade*, to the subject. In *I Love Jam*, I have included some of my favorites to get your imagination going. Ranging from a classic Italian jam tart that you can adapt to fit any jam or marmalade idling in your pantry to an unusual plum jam–enhanced beet soup, the recipes at the end of this book are sure to add zest and sparkle to your culinary repertoire. Not only is homemade jam fantastic on toast, but it is also a surprisingly versatile cooking ingredient. Whether strawberry or orange, melon or fig, the possibilities are endless—and endlessly satisfying.

Let's get jamming!

LEMON MARMALADE

Approximate Yield: ten 8-ounce jars *Shelf Life:* 2 years

Lemons are one of the best fruits for making marmalade. Their high pectin content, natural tartness, and bright, sunny flavor make them particularly easy to work with and well suited to the marmalade process. Lemon marmalade is extremely versatile and can be served as an accompaniment to poultry, used as a secret ingredient in cocktails, or paired with creamy desserts. And, of course, it is excellent on toast, too!

2½ pounds lemons (preferably Lisbon), cut into eighths

2 pounds seeded lemons, halved crosswise, each half cut lengthwise into quarters and sliced crosswise medium-thin

4¼ pounds white cane sugar

¼ to ½ cup strained freshly squeezed lemon juice

DAY 1

Place the lemon eighths in a nonreactive saucepan where they will fit snugly in a single layer. Add enough cold water for the fruit to bob freely. Cover tightly and let rest overnight at room temperature.

DAY 2

Prepare the cooked lemon juice: Bring the pan with the lemon eighths to a boil over high heat, then decrease the heat to medium. Cook the fruit at a lively simmer, covered, for 2 to 3 hours, until the lemons are very soft and the liquid has become slightly syrupy. As the lemons cook, press down on them

Continued

gently with a spoon every 30 minutes or so, adding a little more water if necessary. The water level should stay consistently high enough for the fruit to remain submerged and float freely as it cooks.

When the lemons are finished cooking, strain their juice by pouring the hot fruit and liquid into a medium strainer or colander suspended over a heatproof storage container or nonreactive saucepan. Cover the entire setup well with plastic wrap and let drip overnight at room temperature.

Meanwhile, prepare the sliced lemons: Place the slices in a wide stainless-steel kettle and cover amply with cold water. Bring to a boil over high heat, then decrease the heat and simmer for 5 minutes. Drain, discarding the liquid. Return the lemon slices to the kettle and cover with 1 inch cold water. Bring to a boil over high heat, decrease the heat to medium, and cook at a lively simmer, covered, for 30 to 40 minutes, until the fruit is very tender. As the

fruit cooks, stir it gently every 15 minutes or so, adding a little more water if necessary. The water level should stay consistently high enough for the fruit to remain submerged as it cooks. Remove the pan from the heat, cover tightly, and let rest overnight at room temperature.

DAY 3
Place a saucer with 5 metal teaspoons in a flat place in your freezer for testing the marmalade later.

Remove the plastic wrap from the lemon eighths and their juice and discard the lemons. Strain the juice well through a very fine-mesh strainer to remove any lingering solids.

In a large mixing bowl, combine the sugar, cooked lemon juice, and lemon slices and their liquid. Stir well. Dip a small spoon into the syrupy liquid and taste the liquid. If you do not detect a bright, tart lemon flavor, cautiously add a little fresh lemon juice, stirring and tasting as you go, until you can just taste the tartness and lemon flavor of the juice in the mixture. Once you have reached this point, the mixture is ready to cook.

Transfer the mixture to an 11-quart or 12-quart copper preserving pan or a wide nonreactive kettle.

Bring the mixture to a boil over high heat. Cook at a rapid boil until the setting point is reached; this will take a minimum of 25 minutes, but may take longer depending on your individual stove and pan. Initially, the mixture will bubble gently for several minutes; then, as more moisture cooks out of it and its sugar concentration increases, it will begin foaming. Do not stir it at all during the initial bubbling; then, once it starts to foam, stir it gently every few minutes with a heatproof rubber spatula. As it gets close to being done, stir it slowly every minute or two to prevent burning, decreasing the heat a tiny bit if necessary. The marmalade is ready for testing when its color darkens slightly and its bubbles become very small.

To test the marmalade for doneness, remove it from the heat and carefully transfer a representative half-spoonful to one of your frozen spoons. It should look shiny, with tiny bubbles throughout. Replace the spoon in the freezer for 3 to 4 minutes, then remove and carefully feel the underside of the spoon. It should be neither warm nor cold; if still warm, return it to the freezer for a moment. Tilt the spoon vertically to see whether the marmalade runs; if it does not run, and if its top layer has thickened to a jelly consistency, it is done. If it runs, cook it for another few minutes, stirring, and test again as needed.

When the marmalade has finished cooking, turn off the heat but do not stir. Using a stainless-steel spoon, skim off any surface foam and discard. Pour the marmalade into sterilized jars and process according to the manufacturer's instructions or as directed on page xiv.

Continued

Variations:

MEYER LEMON MARMALADE

Replace the Lisbon lemon slices with Meyer lemon slices, but do not simmer the slices on Day 2. Instead, only slice and soak them on Day 2. Then, on Day 3, simmer the slices very briefly until tender (they can take as little as 5 minutes to become soft). Proceed with the rest of the recipe as directed.

BOURBON'D LEMON MARMALADE

Replace 1½ pounds of the white cane sugar with dark brown cane sugar. When you are ready to cook the marmalade, add a large pinch of kosher salt and several gratings of fresh nutmeg to the marmalade mixture. Proceed with the rest of the recipe as directed. When the marmalade is done cooking, stir in ¼ to ⅓ cup bourbon.

ENGLISH MARMALADE

Approximate Yield: eight 8-ounce jars *Shelf Life:* 2 years

If you are a die-hard marmalade lover whose vision of marmalade resembles an ultra-thick-cut, treacly preserve redolent of wintry spice, this is the marmalade for you. Nothing quite matches its dark and very bitter flavor. Try it in Fruited Irish Brown Bread (page 63) for a special treat.

1½ pounds Seville oranges, cut into eighths

2½ pounds seeded Seville oranges, halved crosswise,
each half cut lengthwise into quarters and sliced thickly crosswise

2¼ pounds white cane sugar

2¼ pounds light brown cane sugar

4 star anise

¼ to ½ cup strained freshly squeezed lemon juice

Generous splash of bourbon

DAY 1

Place the orange eighths in a nonreactive kettle where they will fit snugly in a single layer. Add enough cold water for the fruit to bob freely. Cover tightly and let rest overnight at room temperature.

Place the orange slices in a second large nonreactive kettle and add water to cover the tops of the fruit by 2 inches. Cover the kettle tightly and let rest overnight at room temperature.

Continued

DAY 2

Bring both kettles to a boil, then decrease the heat to a lively simmer.

Cook the orange eighths, covered, for 3 hours, or until they are very soft and their liquid has become slightly syrupy.

Cook the orange slices, covered, for 2 to 3 hours, until the rinds are very tender. As the fruit cooks, stir it gently every 30 minutes or so, adding a little more water if necessary. The water level should stay consistently high enough in both pans for the fruit to remain submerged and float freely as it cooks.

When the orange eighths have finished cooking, strain their juice by pouring the hot fruit and liquid into a medium strainer or colander suspended over a heatproof storage container or nonreactive saucepan. Cover the entire setup well with plastic wrap and let drip overnight at room temperature. When the orange slices have finished cooking, cover them tightly and let rest overnight at room temperature.

DAY 3

Place a saucer with 5 metal teaspoons in a flat place in your freezer for testing the marmalade later.

Remove the plastic wrap from the orange eighths and their juice and discard the oranges. Strain the juice well through a very fine-mesh strainer to remove any lingering solids.

In a large mixing bowl, combine both sugars, the cooked orange juice, star anise, and orange slices and their liquid. Stir well. Dip a small spoon into the syrupy liquid and taste the liquid. If you do not detect a bright, tart lemon flavor, cautiously add a little lemon juice, stirring and tasting as you go, until you can just taste the tartness and lemon flavor of the juice in the mixture. Once you have reached this point, the mixture is ready to cook.

Transfer the mixture to an 11-quart or 12-quart copper preserving pan or a wide nonreactive kettle.

Continued

Bring the mixture to a boil over high heat. Cook at a rapid boil until the setting point is reached; this will take a minimum of 30 to 45 minutes, but may take longer depending on your individual stove and pan. Initially, the mixture will bubble gently for several minutes; then, as more moisture cooks out of it and its sugar concentration increases, it will begin foaming somewhat. Do not stir it at all during the initial bubbling; then, once it starts to foam, stir it gently every few minutes with a heatproof rubber spatula. After several minutes of foaming, stir in the bourbon. As the marmalade gets close to being done, stir it slowly every minute or two to prevent burning, decreasing the heat a tiny bit if necessary. The marmalade is ready for testing when its color darkens slightly and its bubbles become very small.

To test the marmalade for doneness, remove it from the heat and carefully transfer a representative half-spoonful to one of your frozen spoons. It should look shiny, with tiny bubbles throughout. Replace the spoon in the freezer for 3 to 4 minutes, then remove and carefully feel the underside of the spoon. It should be neither warm nor cold; if still warm, return it to the freezer for a moment. Tilt the spoon vertically to see whether the marmalade runs; if it is reluctant to run, and if its top layer has thickened to a jelly consistency, it is done. If it runs, cook it for another few minutes, stirring, and test again as needed. Be careful not to overcook the marmalade, as it may continue to thicken slightly after it cools.

When the marmalade has finished cooking, turn off the heat but do not stir. Using a stainless-steel spoon, skim off any surface foam and discard. Remove the star anise. Pour the marmalade into sterilized jars and process according to the manufacturer's instructions or as directed on page xiv.

NAVEL ORANGE MARMALADE

Approximate Yield: nine or ten 8-ounce jars *Shelf Life:* 2 years

A sweet orange marmalade is a versatile classic and an essential part of any jam-maker's repertoire. Each variety of sweet orange has its own distinct flavor profile, and different oranges can be switched out at will to create new and exciting marmalades. In this recipe, lemons provide a tart backdrop to the intensity of the oranges, tempering their natural sweetness.

2 pounds lemons (preferably Lisbon), cut into eighths

2 pounds navel oranges, halved crosswise, each half cut lengthwise into quarters and sliced crosswise medium-thin

3½ pounds white cane sugar

½ to 1 cup strained freshly squeezed lemon juice

DAY 1

Place the lemon eighths in a nonreactive saucepan where they will fit snugly in a single layer. Add enough cold water for the fruit to bob freely. Cover tightly and let rest overnight at room temperature.

Place the sliced oranges in a separate nonreactive saucepan and cover with enough water to reach 1 inch above the tops. Cover tightly and let rest overnight at room temperature.

DAY 2

Prepare the cooked lemon juice: Bring the pan with the lemon eighths to a boil over high heat, then decrease the heat to medium. Cook the fruit at a lively simmer, covered, for 2 to 3 hours, until the lemons are very soft and the liquid has become

Continued

slightly syrupy. As the lemons cook, press down on them gently with a spoon every 30 minutes or so, adding a little more water if necessary. The water level should stay consistently high enough for the fruit to remain submerged and float freely as it cooks.

When the lemons are finished cooking, strain their juice by pouring the hot fruit and liquid into a medium strainer or colander suspended over a heatproof storage container or nonreactive saucepan. Cover the entire setup well with plastic wrap and let drip overnight at room temperature.

Meanwhile, prepare the orange slices: Bring the pan with them to a boil over high heat, then decrease the heat to medium and cook, covered, at a lively simmer for 30 to 40 minutes, until the fruit is very tender. If necessary, add a little more water during the cooking; the fruit should remain submerged throughout the cooking process. When the orange slices have finished cooking, remove the pan from the heat, cover tightly, and let rest overnight at room temperature.

DAY 3
Place a saucer with 5 metal teaspoons in a flat place in your freezer for testing the marmalade later.

Remove the plastic wrap from the lemon eighths and their juice and discard the lemons. Strain the juice through a very fine-mesh strainer to remove any lingering solids.

In a large mixing bowl, combine the sugar, cooked lemon juice, and cooked orange slices and their liquid. Stir well. Dip a small spoon into the syrupy liquid and taste the liquid. If you do not detect a bright, tart lemon flavor, cautiously add a little fresh lemon juice, stirring and tasting as you go, until you can just taste the tartness and lemon flavor of the juice in the mixture. Once you have reached this point, the mixture is ready to cook.

Transfer the mixture to an 11-quart or 12-quart copper preserving pan or a wide nonreactive kettle. Bring the mixture to a boil over high heat. Cook at a rapid boil until

Continued

the setting point is reached; this will take a minimum of 30 minutes, but may take longer depending upon your individual stove and pan. Initially, the mixture will bubble gently for several minutes; then, as more moisture cooks out of it and its sugar concentration increases, it will begin foaming. Do not stir it at all during the initial bubbling; then, once it starts to foam, stir it gently every few minutes with a heatproof rubber spatula. As it gets close to being done, stir it slowly every minute or two to prevent burning, decreasing the heat a tiny bit if necessary. The marmalade is ready for testing when its color darkens slightly and its bubbles become very small.

To test the marmalade for doneness, remove it from the heat and carefully transfer a representative half-spoonful of marmalade to one of your frozen spoons. It should look shiny, with tiny bubbles throughout. Replace the spoon in the freezer for 3 to 4 minutes, then remove and carefully feel the underside of the spoon. It should be neither warm nor cold; if still warm, return it to the freezer for a moment. Tilt the spoon vertically to see whether the marmalade runs; if it does not run, and if its top layer has thickened to a jelly consistency, it is done. If it runs, cook it for another few minutes, stirring, and test again as needed.

When the marmalade has finished cooking, turn off the heat but do not stir. Using a stainless-steel spoon, skim off any surface foam and discard. Pour the marmalade into sterilized jars and process according to the manufacturer's instructions or as directed on page xiv.

Variation:
VALENCIA OR BLOOD ORANGE MARMALADE
Substitute Valencia or blood orange slices for the navel orange slices in the recipe. Proceed with the rest of the recipe as directed.

KUMQUAT MARMALADE

Approximate Yield: ten 8-ounce jars *Shelf Life:* 2 years

Kumquats make a gorgeous marmalade; their thin skins make for a lively yet gentle texture. I included three kumquat marmalade recipes in The Blue Chair Jam Cookbook, *but this is the version I prefer for cooking; the kumquat flavor here is clearer and the pieces of kumquat are larger. If you can bear the work of seeding the kumquats, this marmalade will reward you through the whole year, both brightening your breakfast table and livening up savory dishes such as Brussels Sprouts with Kumquats & Smoked Salt (page 67).*

2¼ pounds Eureka or Lisbon lemons, cut into eighths

2¼ pounds tart kumquats (such as Nagami), seeded and quartered

4¼ pounds white cane sugar

¼ to ½ cup strained freshly squeezed lemon juice

DAY 1

Place the lemon eighths in a nonreactive saucepan where they will fit snugly in a single layer. Add enough cold water for the fruit to bob freely. Cover tightly and let rest overnight at room temperature.

DAY 2

Prepare the cooked lemon juice: Bring the lemon eighths to a boil over high heat, then lower the heat to medium. Cook the fruit at a lively simmer, covered, for 2 to 3 hours, until the lemons are very soft and the liquid has become slightly syrupy. As the lemons

Continued

cook, press down on them gently with a spoon every 30 minutes or so, adding a little more water if needed. The water level should stay consistently high enough for the fruit to remain submerged and float freely as it cooks.

When the lemons are finished cooking, strain their juice by pouring the hot fruit and liquid into a medium strainer or colander suspended over a heatproof storage container or nonreactive saucepan. Cover the entire setup well with plastic wrap and let drip overnight at room temperature.

Meanwhile, prepare the kumquats: Place the kumquat quarters in a wide stainless-steel kettle and add cold water to reach 1 inch above the tops. Cover tightly and let rest overnight at room temperature.

DAY 3

Place a saucer with 5 metal teaspoons in a flat place in your freezer for testing the marmalade later.

Bring the pan with the kumquats to a boil over high heat, then decrease the heat to medium and cook, uncovered, at a lively simmer until the fruit is tender, 15 to 30 minutes.

Remove the plastic wrap from the lemon eighths and their juice and discard the lemons. Strain the juice well through a very fine-mesh sieve to remove any lingering solids.

In a large bowl, combine the sugar, cooked lemon juice, kumquats and their liquid, and ¼ cup of the fresh lemon juice. Stir well. Dip a small spoon into the syrupy liquid and taste the liquid. If you do not detect a bright, tart lemon flavor, cautiously add a little bit more lemon juice, stirring and tasting as you go, until you can just taste the tartness and lemon flavor of the juice in the mixture. Once you have reached this point, the mixture is ready to cook.

Continued

Transfer the mixture to an 11-quart or 12-quart copper preserving pan or wide nonreactive kettle. Bring the mixture to a boil over high heat. Cook at a rapid boil until the setting point is reached; this will take a minimum of 25 minutes but may take longer, depending on your individual stove and pan. Initially, the mixture will bubble gently for several minutes; then, as more moisture cooks out of it and the sugar concentration increases, it will begin foaming. Do not stir it at all during the initial bubbling; then, once it starts to foam, stir it gently every few minutes with a heatproof rubber spatula. As it gets close to being done, stir it frequently to prevent burning, lowering the heat a tiny bit if needed. The marmalade is ready for testing when its color darkens slightly and its bubbles become very small.

To test the marmalade for doneness, remove it from the heat and carefully transfer a representative half-spoonful to one of your frozen spoons. It should look shiny, with tiny bubbles throughout. Place the spoon back in the freezer for 3 to 4 minutes, then remove and carefully feel the underside of the spoon. It should be neither warm nor cold; if still warm, return it to the freezer for a moment. Tilt the spoon vertically to see whether the marmalade runs; if it does not run, and if its top layer has thickened to a jelly consistency, it is done. If it runs, cook it for another few minutes, stirring, and test again as needed.

Turn off the heat but do not stir. Using a stainless-steel spoon, skim off any surface foam and discard. Pour the marmalade into sterilized jars and process according to the manufacturer's instructions or as directed on page xiv.

RHUBARB JAM

Approximate Yield: six or seven 8-ounce jars   *Shelf Life:* 6 months

One thing that always mystifies me is the difficulty of finding rhubarb cooked on its own; we always seem to succumb to the temptation to combine it with something else. Yet rhubarb's unique flavor and texture set it apart from other early-summer ingredients, and a really perfect plain rhubarb jam is hard to beat. For a simple British after-dinner treat, fold rhubarb jam into lightly whipped cream to make a refreshing, summery fool.

4 pounds trimmed rhubarb stalks, cut into 3- to 4-inch lengths

2¾ pounds white cane sugar

3 ounces strained freshly squeezed lemon juice

Scant ⅛ teaspoon citric acid

Scant ⅛ teaspoon ascorbic acid

Place a saucer with 5 metal teaspoons in a flat place in your freezer for testing the jam later.

Combine the rhubarb, sugar, lemon juice, and citric and ascorbic acids in an 11-quart or 12-quart copper preserving pan or a wide stainless-steel kettle. Heat slowly, stirring with a large heatproof rubber spatula, until the sugar is dissolving and the rhubarb begins releasing a lot of juice. Turn the heat up to high and boil, stirring frequently and gradually decreasing the heat if the jam starts to stick, until thickened and no longer watery, about 20 minutes. For the last 5 to 10 minutes of cooking, you will need to stir the jam nearly constantly to keep it from sticking.

Continued

When the jam has thickened, test it for doneness. To test, carefully transfer a representative half-spoonful of jam to one of your frozen spoons. Replace the spoon in the freezer for 3 to 4 minutes, then remove and carefully feel the underside of the spoon. It should be neither warm nor cold; if still warm, return it to the freezer for a moment. Tilt the spoon vertically to see how quickly the jam runs; if it runs slowly, and if it has thickened to a gloppy consistency, it is done. If it runs very quickly or appears watery, cook it for another few minutes, stirring, and test again as needed. This jam, while spreadable, has a relatively loose texture.

Turn off the heat but do not stir. Using a stainless-steel spoon, skim any foam from the surface of the jam. Pour the jam into sterilized jars and process according to the manufacturer's instructions or as directed on page xiv.

Variation:
RHUBARB JAM WITH VANILLA & DRIED CHERRIES
Add a large handful of dried cherries and one 1½-inch piece vanilla bean, split and scraped, to the jam mixture at the start of cooking. Proceed with the recipe as directed. When the jam is done cooking, remove the vanilla bean.

STRAWBERRY JAM

Approximate Yield: six or seven 8-ounce jars *Shelf Life:* 6 to 8 months

Strawberry jam is perhaps the most classic of all jams, yet it can be challenging to find a truly great one. In this recipe, the berries are macerated for a week to draw out their juices and deepen their flavor before the cooking process begins. Lemon juice tempers the natural sweetness of the berries and pushes the fruit's flavor forward. Though we always think of strawberry jam for toast, it also makes a lovely tart filling, as in Alessandra's Crostata (page 80).

4 pounds hulled fresh strawberries

¼ cup plus about ⅔ cup strained freshly squeezed lemon juice

Scant ⅛ teaspoon citric acid

Scant 1⅛ teaspoon ascorbic acid

2½ pounds white cane sugar

DAY 1

Place the strawberries in a large glass or hard plastic storage container. In a glass measuring cup, mix ¼ cup of the lemon juice with the citric and ascorbic acids, stirring well to dissolve the acids. Pour the sugar evenly over the fruit, then pour the lemon juice mixture over the sugar-fruit mixture. Do not stir. Cover tightly and place in the refrigerator. Leave to macerate for 7 days, stirring once every day or two.

1 WEEK LATER

Place a saucer with 5 metal teaspoons in a flat place in your freezer for testing the jam later.

Continued

Remove the strawberry mixture from the refrigerator and stir in half of the remaining ⅔ cup lemon juice. Dip a small spoon into the liquidy part of the mixture and taste for lemon juice. If you do not detect any lemon, cautiously add a little more juice, stirring and tasting as you go, until you can just taste the tartness and lemon flavor of the juice in the mixture. Once you have reached this point, the mixture is ready to cook.

Transfer the mixture to an 11-quart or 12-quart copper preserving pan or a wide nonreactive kettle. Bring the mixture to a boil over high heat, stirring occasionally with a large heatproof rubber spatula. Boil, stirring frequently, for 4 minutes. Remove from the heat and, using a large stainless-steel spoon, skim the stiff foam from the top of the mixture and discard. Return the jam to a boil, then decrease the heat slightly. Continue to cook, monitoring the heat closely, until the jam thickens, 30 to 35 minutes. Scrape the bottom of the pan often with your spatula, and decrease the heat gradually as more and more moisture cooks out of the jam. For the last 10 to 15 minutes of cooking, stir the jam slowly and frequently to keep it from scorching.

When the jam seems ready, test it for doneness. To test, remove the jam from the heat and carefully transfer a representative half-spoonful of jam to one of your frozen spoons. Place the spoon back in the freezer for 3 to 4 minutes, then remove and carefully feel the underside of the spoon. It should be neither warm nor cold; if still warm, return it to the freezer for a moment. Tilt the spoon vertically to see how quickly the jam runs; if it runs slowly, and if it has thickened to a jammy consistency, it is done. If it runs very quickly or appears watery, cook it for another few minutes, stirring, and test again as needed.

Turn off the heat but do not stir. Using a stainless-steel spoon, skim any foam from the surface of the jam. Pour the jam into sterilized jars and process according to the manufacturer's instructions or as directed on page xiv.

Continued

Variations:

STRAWBERRY-ROSE JAM

Add one 1½-inch piece vanilla bean, split and scraped, to the jam mixture at the start of the cooking. When the jam is done cooking, remove the vanilla bean and add a small splash of kirsch. Add a small splash of rosewater. Carefully taste the jam and add a few more drops of rosewater and/or kirsch, as necessary, keeping in mind that their flavor will be slightly milder once the jam has cooled.

STRAWBERRY JAM WITH AGED BALSAMIC & BLACK PEPPER

Add 2 to 3 tablespoons aged balsamic vinegar to the jam mixture at the start of cooking. Cook the jam as directed. When the jam is done cooking, add several grinds of black pepper to the jam, carefully tasting as you go. The pepper flavor should be present but not overpowering.

STRAWBERRY-MARSALA JAM WITH ROSEMARY

Cook the jam as directed. When the jam is done cooking, stir in 1 to 2 ounces sweet or medium-sweet Marsala. Place three or four (6-inch) sprigs rosemary into the jam and let steep for a few minutes off the heat. Carefully taste the jam and either remove the sprigs or leave them in for another minute or two, keeping in mind that their flavor will be slightly milder once the jam has cooled. Using tongs, discard the rosemary.

APRICOT JAM

Approximate Yield: nine 8-ounce jars *Shelf Life:* 6 to 8 months

This excellent apricot jam includes the kernels from the apricot pits to accentuate the naturally almondy notes of the fruit. Apricot pairs well with countless other flavors; for a few ideas to get you started, see the recipe variations below.

5 pounds pitted and halved apricots, pits reserved

1 cup strained freshly squeezed lemon juice

Scant ⅛ teaspoon citric acid

Scant ⅛ teaspoon ascorbic acid

2½ pounds white cane sugar

DAY 1

Place the apricots in a large glass or hard plastic storage container. In a glass measuring cup, mix ½ cup of the lemon juice with the citric and ascorbic acids, stirring well to dissolve the acid. Pour the lemon juice mixture over the apricots and stir to combine. Pour the sugar evenly over the fruit. Press a sheet of plastic wrap directly onto the surface of the mixture, smoothing well to minimize air bubbles (this will help keep the fruit from browning as it sits). Cover tightly and place in the refrigerator. Leave to macerate for 7 days, stirring once every day or two and replacing the plastic wrap each time you stir.

1 WEEK LATER

Place a saucer with 5 metal teaspoons in a flat place in your freezer for testing the jam later.

Continued

Place several apricot pits on the floor between two old, clean cloths and, using a hammer, tap them through the top cloth until they crack. Carefully remove the almond-like kernel from each pit, discarding the shells, until you have enough to make 1 heaping tablespoon chopped. Place the chopped kernels in a fine-mesh stainless-steel tea infuser with a firm latch and set aside.

Remove the apricot mixture from the refrigerator and stir in half of the remaining ½ cup lemon juice. Dip a small spoon into the liquidy part of the mixture and taste for lemon juice. If you do not detect any lemon, cautiously add a little more juice, stirring and tasting as you go, until you can just taste the tartness and lemon flavor of the juice in the mixture. Once you have reached this point, the mixture is ready to cook.

Transfer the mixture to an 11-quart or 12-quart copper preserving pan or a wide nonreactive kettle. Place the tea infuser into the mixture, pressing down on it to submerge it. Bring the mixture to a boil over high heat, stirring occasionally with a large heatproof rubber spatula. Boil, stirring

frequently, for 4 minutes. Remove from the heat and, using a large stainless-steel spoon, skim the stiff foam from the top of the mixture and discard. Return the jam to a boil, then decrease the heat slightly. Continue to cook, monitoring the heat closely, until the jam thickens, 30 to 40 minutes. Scrape the bottom of the pan often with your spatula, and decrease the heat gradually as more and more moisture cooks out of the jam. For the last 10 to 15 minutes of cooking, stir the jam slowly and frequently to keep it from scorching.

When the jam seems ready, test it for doneness. To test, remove the jam from the heat and carefully transfer a representative half-spoonful of jam to one of your frozen spoons. Place the spoon back in the freezer for 3 to 4 minutes, then remove and carefully feel the underside of the spoon. It should be neither warm nor cold; if still warm, return it to the freezer for a moment. Tilt the spoon vertically to see how quickly the jam runs; if it runs slowly, and if it has thickened to a gloppy consistency, it is done. If it runs very quickly or appears watery, cook it for another few minutes, stirring, and test again as needed.

Turn off the heat but do not stir. Remove the tea ball of kernels. Using a stainless-steel spoon, skim any foam from the surface of the jam. Pour the jam into sterilized jars and process according to the manufacturer's instructions or as directed on page xiv.

Variation:
APRICOT JAM WITH ROSE, SAFFRON, OR CARDAMOM

Apricot jam is delicious flavored with rosewater, saffron, cardamom, or any combination thereof. To flavor your apricot jam with rosewater, add 2 or 3 small splashes of rosewater to the finished jam at the end of cooking, stir well, and carefully taste. Add more rosewater judiciously, tasting carefully as you go, until the rose flavor is present but not overpowering. To flavor your jam with saffron, add a medium pinch of saffron threads to the jam at the start of cooking. To flavor with cardamom, add 1 tablespoon lightly crushed green cardamom pods to the apricot kernels in the mesh tea infuser and proceed with the recipe as directed.

BLACKBERRY JAM

Approximate Yield: five 8-ounce jars *Shelf Life:* 6 to 8 months

This is one of the most summery jams and also one of the simplest to make. There is something about its dark flavor that always delights me. Once you have mastered the basic technique, you can try the variations with different fruits below. This recipe yields a pie-like result that keeps much of the fruit's original integrity intact; it will work beautifully with any good blackberry variety.

3½ pounds fresh midsummer blackberries

1¾ pounds white cane sugar

3 ounces strained freshly squeezed lemon juice

Place a saucer with 5 metal teaspoons in a flat place in your freezer for testing the jam later.

Combine the berries, sugar, and lemon juice in an 11-quart or 12-quart copper preserving pan or a wide stainless-steel kettle. Heat slowly, stirring with a large heatproof rubber spatula, until the sugar is dissolving and the berries begin releasing a lot of juice. Turn the heat up to high and cook, stirring frequently. Test the jam for doneness 15 to 20 minutes from the time it reaches a rolling boil.

To test for doneness, carefully transfer a representative half-spoonful of jam to one of your frozen spoons. Replace the spoon in the freezer for 3 to 4 minutes, then remove and carefully feel the underside of the spoon. It should be neither warm nor cold; if still warm, return it to the freezer for a moment. Tilt the spoon vertically to see whether the jam runs; if it just refuses to run, and if it has thickened to a near-jelly consistency, it is done. If it runs, cook it for another few minutes, stirring, and test again as needed.

Using a stainless-steel spoon, skim any remaining foam from the surface of the jam. Pour the jam into sterilized jars and process according to the manufacturer's instructions or as directed on page xiv.

Variations:

BLACKBERRY JAM WITH LEMON BASIL OR LEMON VERBENA

Cook the jam as directed. At the end of cooking, place a small bunch of fresh lemon basil or lemon verbena into the jam and let steep for 1 to 2 minutes off the heat. Stir and carefully taste the jam, and either remove the herbs or leave them in for another minute or two; their flavor should be subtle, but keep in mind that it will mellow slightly as the jam cools. Using tongs, discard the herbs.

BOYSENBERRY JAM

Replace the blackberries with boysenberries, dividing the boysenberries into one 1½-pound and one 2-pound quantity. To cook the jam, combine the 1½ pounds berries with the sugar and lemon juice. Cook as directed. Once the mixture reaches a rolling boil, boil it vigorously for 5 minutes, stirring frequently. After 5 minutes, add the remaining 2 pounds of boysenberries, stirring well to combine. Over high heat, bring the mixture back to a boil, stirring every 30 seconds or so. Once it reaches a boil, cook it for 10 to 15 minutes more, stirring frequently. Begin testing for doneness after 10 minutes.

BLACK & BLUEBERRY JAM

Replace 1¾ pounds of the blackberries with 1¾ pounds blueberries; tarter blueberries are best. Add a pinch of apple pie spice to the jam at the beginning of cooking. Proceed with the rest of the recipe as directed.

BLACK MISSION FIG JAM

Approximate Yield: nine 8-ounce jars *Shelf Life:* 2 years

This is the most stellar plain fig jam out there, and it is very easy to make. For great results, be sure to use the most flavorful thin-skinned Black Mission figs you can find, at the height of their season. Figs typically have two harvests, one in early summer and one in early fall. If you can bear to wait, the second harvest is always the best; by the end of summer, the figs have grown denser, with that uniquely earthy quality that is their hallmark. Unlike many fig jams, this jam contains whole pieces of fruit and is not overly sweet. Fig jam pairs especially well with cheese and is an essential ingredient in Black Sesame–Fig Ice Cream (page 84).

2½ pounds plus 2½ pounds whole stemmed Black Mission figs

2½ pounds white cane sugar

½ to ⅔ cup strained freshly squeezed lemon juice

Several drops of green Chartreuse

Several drops of Bénédictine

Place a saucer with 5 metal teaspoons in a flat place in your freezer for testing the jam later.

Using an immersion blender and a large bowl or a food processor fitted with a metal blade, purée 2½ pounds whole figs until smooth and transfer to a very large ceramic or stainless-steel bowl.

Quarter the remaining 2½ pounds figs lengthwise and then cut each quarter crosswise into 2 or 3 pieces, depending on the size of the figs. Add them to the fig purée along with the sugar and ½ cup of the lemon juice. Dip a small spoon into the mixture and taste. If you do not detect a bright, tart lemony flavor, cautiously add a little bit more lemon juice, stirring and tasting as you go, until you can just taste the tartness and lemon flavor of the juice in the mixture. Stir in several drops of Chartreuse and Bénédictine: Their flavors should be subtle and accent the figs.

Transfer the mixture to an 11-quart or 12-quart copper preserving pan or wide nonreactive kettle. Bring the mixture to a boil over medium-high heat, stirring very frequently (fig jam tends to stick), and cook, stirring often, until the jam has thickened and appears shiny and any obvious excess liquid has cooked away, 15 to 20 minutes. At this point, test the jam for doneness.

To test, remove the jam from the heat and carefully transfer a representative half-spoonful to one of your frozen spoons. Place the spoon back in the freezer for 3 to 4 minutes, then remove and carefully feel the underside of the spoon. It should be neither warm nor cold; if still warm, return it to the freezer for a moment. Nudge the jam gently with your finger, then tilt the spoon vertically to see how quickly the jam runs; if it runs slowly, and if it has thickened to a gloppy consistency, it is done. If it runs very quickly or appears watery, cook it for another few minutes, stirring, and test again as needed.

Pour the jam into sterilized jars and process according to the manufacturer's instructions or as directed on page xiv.

PLUM JAM

Approximate Yield: seven or eight 8-ounce jars *Shelf Life:* 1 year

Plums make one of the most satisfying and useful of jams, and each variety of plum yields a completely different flavor. The tartness and the pectin hiding in the plums' skins are released and greatly intensified through the cooking process. For a classic British flavor, try Damsons or Greengages, both excellent English varieties. For a more California flavor, try Santa Rosa plums or Flavor King pluots. In addition to being the perfect morning jam, plum jam is a wonderful secret weapon for your cooking pantry, lending not only fruitiness but also tartness, viscosity, and acidity to sauces, braises, and soups. Beet Soup with Plums and Coriander Yogurt (page 68) is a perfect place to start.

5 pounds pitted and halved ripe plums

1 cup strained freshly squeezed lemon juice

Scant ⅛ teaspoon citric acid

Scant ⅛ teaspoon ascorbic acid

2½ pounds white cane sugar

DAY 1

Place the plums in a large glass or hard plastic storage container. In a glass measuring cup, mix ½ cup of the lemon juice with the citric and ascorbic acids, stirring well to dissolve the acid. Pour the sugar evenly over the fruit. Press a sheet of plastic wrap directly onto the surface of the mixture, smoothing well to minimize air bubbles (this will help keep the fruit from browning as it sits).

Cover tightly and place in the refrigerator. Leave to macerate for 7 days, stirring once every day or two and replacing the plastic wrap each time you stir.

1 WEEK LATER
Place a saucer with 5 metal teaspoons in a flat place in your freezer for testing the jam later.

Remove the plum mixture from the refrigerator and stir in half of the remaining ½ cup lemon juice. Dip a small spoon into the liquidy part of the mixture and taste for lemon juice. If you do not detect any lemon, cautiously add a little more juice, stirring and tasting as you go, until you can just taste the tartness and lemon flavor of the juice in the mixture. Once you have reached this point, the mixture is ready to cook.

Transfer the mixture to an 11-quart or 12-quart copper preserving pan or a wide nonreactive kettle. Bring the mixture to a boil over high heat, stirring occasionally with a large heatproof rubber spatula.

Boil, stirring frequently, for 4 minutes. Remove from the heat and, using a large stainless-steel spoon, skim the stiff foam from the top of the mixture and discard. Return the jam to a boil, then decrease the heat slightly. Continue to cook, monitoring the heat closely, until the jam thickens, 30 to 40 minutes. Scrape the bottom of the pan often with your spatula, and decrease the heat gradually as more and more moisture cooks out of the jam. For the last 10 to 15 minutes of cooking, stir the jam slowly and frequently to keep it from scorching.

When the jam seems ready, test it for doneness. To test, remove the jam from the heat and carefully transfer a representative half-spoonful of jam to one of your frozen spoons. Place the spoon back in the freezer for 3 to 4 minutes, then remove and carefully feel the underside of the spoon. It should be neither warm nor cold; if still warm, return it to the freezer for a moment. Tilt the spoon vertically to see how quickly the jam runs; if it runs slowly, and if it has thickened to a

Continued

gloppy consistency, it is done. If it runs very quickly or appears watery, cook it for another few minutes, stirring, and test again as needed.

Turn off the heat but do not stir. Using a stainless-steel spoon, skim any foam from the surface of the jam. Pour the jam into sterilized jars and process according to the manufacturer's instructions or as directed on page xiv.

Variation:
CHERRY-PLUM JAM
Replace 2½ pounds of the plums with 2½ pounds pitted Bing cherries. Proceed with the recipe as directed. When the jam is done cooking, stir in a small splash of kirsch.

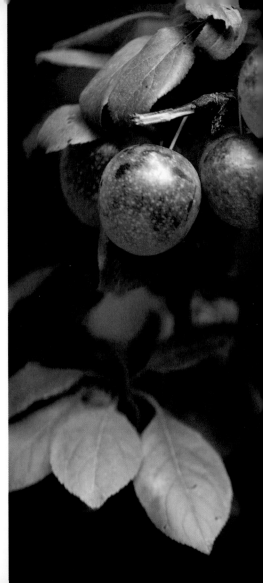

WHITE CHERRY & PEACH JAM

Approximate Yield: six 8-ounce jars *Shelf Life:* 1 year

This jam's perfect balance of flavors and lively texture makes it stand out. With its warm color and flecks of vanilla bean, this preserve is an unusual and delicious use for Rainier cherries. Because Rainiers hold their shape during the cooking process, they are best used for jam in combination with peaches or another fruit. This is a dessert-like jam that is best enjoyed as part of a weekend breakfast or over ice cream in the evening.

2½ pounds peeled early-season yellow peaches (see Note, page 49)

2½ pounds pitted Rainier or other white cherries

2 pounds 2 ounces white cane sugar

½ to ¾ cup strained freshly squeezed lemon juice

Scant ⅛ teaspoon citric acid

Scant ⅛ teaspoon ascorbic acid

Several drops of pure almond extract

Several drops of maraschino liqueur

1 (1-inch) piece vanilla bean, split

Place a saucer with 5 metal teaspoons in a flat place in your freezer for testing the jam later.

Place a cutting board on a rimmed baking sheet or sheet pan. Put the peaches on the board and, using a paring knife, cut enough flesh off the pits to make 2 pounds of prepared fruit. You should end up with pieces of all different shapes and sizes. When you are finished, discard the peach pits.

Place the peach pieces and their collected juices from the baking sheet with the cherries, sugar, ½ cup of the lemon juice, and the citric and ascorbic acids in a large mixing bowl. Stir well to combine. Dip a small spoon into the liquidy part of the mixture and taste for lemon juice. If you do not detect any lemon, cautiously add a little more juice, stirring and tasting as you go, until you can just taste the tartness and lemon flavor of the juice in the mixture. Once this point has been reached, add a few drops each of almond extract and maraschino liqueur. Taste, add a drop or two more of the flavorings if necessary, and add the vanilla bean. Transfer the mixture to an 11-quart or 12-quart copper preserving pan or a wide nonreactive kettle.

Place the jam mixture over high heat and bring it to a boil, stirring every couple of minutes or so. Continue to cook, monitoring the heat closely, until the jam thickens, 25 to 30 minutes. Scrape the bottom of the pan often with your spatula, and decrease the heat gradually

as more and more moisture cooks out of the jam. For the last 10 to 15 minutes of cooking, stir the jam slowly and steadily to keep it from scorching. Skim any stiff foam from the surface of the jam as it cooks and discard.

When the jam has thickened and appears glossy, test it for doneness. To test, carefully transfer a representative half-spoonful of jam to one of your frozen spoons. Replace the spoon in the freezer for 3 to 4 minutes, then remove and carefully feel the underside of the spoon. It should be neither warm nor cold; if still warm, return it to the freezer for a moment. Tilt the spoon vertically to see how quickly the jam runs; if it is reluctant to run, and if it has thickened to a gloppy consistency, it is done. If it runs very quickly or appears watery, cook it for another few minutes, stirring, and test again as needed. While you are waiting for the jam in the freezer to cool, skim off any white foam that appears on the surface of the jam in the pan.

When the jam is ready, remove the vanilla bean. Pour it into sterilized jars and process according to the manufacturer's instructions or as directed on page xiv.

MY RASPBERRY JAM

Approximate Yield: six or seven 8-ounce jars *Shelf Life:* 1 year

This recipe is equally delicious made with either golden or red raspberries; their flavors resemble each other very closely. It is beautiful to look at either way, with the little berries suspended in it, but it is particularly lovely with goldens. Raspberry jam is one of the most delicious jams for toast, but it can also liven up salad dressings, fill layer cakes, and add an extra shot of brightness to summer berry salads.

2 pounds plus 1 pound fresh red or golden raspberries

3 pounds white cane sugar

Place a saucer with 5 metal teaspoons in a flat place in your freezer for testing the jam later.

Combine 2 pounds of the berries with the sugar in an 11-quart or 12-quart copper preserving pan or a wide nonreactive kettle. Place the pan over medium-low heat and cook, stirring and mashing constantly with a heatproof rubber spatula, until the juice begins to run from the berries. As soon as the sugar dissolves, increase the heat to high. Continue to cook, stirring very frequently, until the mixture boils. Boil the mixture vigorously for exactly 12 minutes, stirring frequently. At 12 minutes, quickly stir in the remaining 1 pound of raspberries; cook, stirring frequently and carefully so as not to break the berries, until they just turn translucent but still hold their shape, 1 to 3 more minutes. At this point, test the jam for doneness.

Continued

To test, carefully transfer a representative half-spoonful of jam to one of your frozen spoons. Replace the spoon in the freezer for 3 to 4 minutes, then remove and carefully feel the underside of the spoon. It should be neither warm nor cold; if still warm, return it to the freezer for a moment. Tilt the spoon vertically to see whether the jam runs; if it does not run, and if it has thickened to a near-jelly consistency, it is done. If it runs, cook it for another minute or two, stirring, and test again as needed.

Using a stainless-steel spoon, skim any remaining foam from the surface of the jam. Pour the jam into sterilized jars and process according to the manufacturer's instructions or as directed on page xiv.

Variation:

RED RASPBERRY JAM WITH ROSE GERANIUM

For this classic variation, rinse two 10-inch sprigs of rose geranium leaves well under cold water, pat them dry between two clean kitchen towels, and set them aside while you cook the jam as directed. When the cooking is completed, rub the rose geranium sprigs briefly between your fingers to release their oils, place them into the jam, and let them steep for a minute or two off the heat. Taste carefully and either remove the sprigs or leave them in for another minute or two, keeping in mind that the rose geranium flavor will be slightly milder once the jam has cooled. When the flavor is strong enough for your liking, use tongs to discard the sprigs and pour the jam into jars as directed.

MELON JAM

Approximate Yield: six 8-ounce jars *Shelf Life:* 1 year

Melon jams, though commonly found in France, are rare in this country. A good melon jam is a truly surprising and delectable treat. The important thing is the melon itself: It must be highly flavorful, aromatic, and perfectly buttery and ripe. A tender peachy-fleshed variety of muskmelon is best for this jam. Melon jam makes a wonderful partner for yogurt.

1 pound plus 1 pound white cane sugar

⅓ ounce plus ⅓ ounce powdered apple pectin

2 pounds 15 ounces seeded and skinned Crenshaw or other flavorful peachy-fleshed muskmelon, sliced into pieces about ¼ inch thick by ⅝ inch wide by 1 inch long

3 pounds 5 ounces seeded and skinned Crenshaw melon, cut into 2-inch chunks

½ to ¾ cup strained freshly squeezed lemon juice

DAY 1

Have ready two large glass or hard plastic storage containers with tight-fitting lids.

In a bowl, combine 1 pound of the sugar with ⅓ ounce of the pectin and whisk well to evenly distribute the pectin granules throughout the sugar. Place the sliced melon in one of the storage containers and pour the sugar-pectin mixture over the fruit, stirring the fruit as you pour to prevent the pectin from clumping.

Continued

In the same bowl, combine the remaining 1 pound sugar with the remaining ⅓ ounce pectin, whisking well. Place the melon chunks in the second storage container and pour the sugar-pectin mixture over the fruit, stirring as you pour. Cover both containers and let macerate in the refrigerator for 48 hours.

2 DAYS LATER

Place a saucer with 5 metal teaspoons in a flat place in your freezer for testing the jam later.

Remove the melon from the refrigerator. Put the melon chunks through the fine holes of a food mill and add them to the sliced melon. Scrape any solids that will not go through the food mill back into the jam mixture, breaking up the chunks as you go. Add ½ cup of the lemon juice and stir well to combine. Dip a small spoon into the liquidy part of the mixture and taste for lemon juice. If you do not detect any lemon, cautiously add a little more juice, stirring and tasting as

you go, until you can just taste the tartness and lemon flavor of the juice in the mixture. Once you have reached this point, the mixture is ready to cook.

Transfer the mixture to an 11-quart or 12-quart copper preserving pan or a wide nonreactive kettle.

Bring the jam mixture to a boil over high heat, stirring occasionally with a large heatproof rubber spatula. Cook, stirring frequently and decreasing the heat slightly if you detect any sticking, for 60 to 70 minutes, until the jam has thickened and any hint of wateriness has gone. As the jam cooks, use a stainless-steel spoon to skim off any stiff surface foam and discard. If you are using a firmer variety, such as Charentais, you may wish to mash the fruit partway through the cooking process with a potato masher to help it along; if you are using Crenshaw or another softer variety, this should not be necessary.

To test the jam for doneness, carefully transfer a representative half-spoonful to one of your frozen spoons. Replace the spoon in the freezer for 3 to 4 minutes, then remove and carefully feel the underside of the spoon. It should be neither warm nor cold; if still warm, return it to the freezer for a moment. Tilt the spoon vertically to see how quickly the jam runs; if it runs very slowly, and if it has thickened to a gloppy consistency, it is done. If it runs very quickly or appears watery, cook it for another few minutes, stirring, and test again as needed.

Turn off the heat but do not stir. Using a stainless-steel spoon, skim any remaining foam from the surface of the jam. Pour the jam into sterilized jars and process according to the manufacturer's instructions or as directed on page xiv.

PEACH JAM

Approximate Yield: twelve 8-ounce jars *Shelf Life:* 8 months

Rich late-season peaches plus peach kernels and leaves: the last word in peach jam. The final peaches of summer are large, dense, and bursting with flavor. Peach kernels bring out the fruit's almondy side, and the leaves impart an immediately recognizable flavor that is at once peachy, almondy, and green. Because this jam uses all parts of the fruit, its flavor is both extra-peachy and unexpectedly complex.

6½ pounds large ripe yellow or white freestone peaches, peeled (see Note)

½ to ¾ cup strained freshly squeezed lemon juice

Scant ⅛ teaspoon citric acid

Scant ⅛ teaspoon ascorbic acid

2¾ pounds white cane sugar

3 or 4 (12-inch) sprigs yellow peach leaves

DAY 1

Prepare the peaches: Place a cutting board on a rimmed baking sheet to catch any juice that may run from the fruit. Place the peeled peaches on the board, halve them lengthwise, and pit them, reserving and refrigerating the pits. Cut enough of the peaches into slices about ⅓ inch thick to make 5½ pounds of prepared fruit and juices. Transfer the sliced peaches and their juices to a hard plastic or glass storage container. In a glass measuring cup, mix ½ cup of the lemon juice with the citric and ascorbic acids, stirring well to dissolve the acid. Pour the lemon juice mixture over the peaches and stir to combine. Pour the sugar evenly over the fruit. Press a sheet of plastic wrap directly onto the surface of the mixture, smoothing well to minimize air bubbles (this will help keep the fruit from browning as it sits). Cover tightly and place in the refrigerator. Leave to macerate for 7 days, stirring once every day or two and replacing the plastic wrap each time you stir.

1 WEEK LATER

Place a saucer with 5 metal teaspoons in a flat place in your freezer for testing the jam later. Rinse the peach sprigs well under cold water, pat them dry between two clean kitchen towels, and set aside.

Remove the peach pits from the refrigerator. Place several pits on the floor between two old, clean cloths. Using a hammer, tap each pit through the top cloth a few times to crack it. Carefully remove the almond-like kernel from inside each pit until you have enough kernels to make 1 tablespoon coarsely chopped. Discard the shells and remaining pits. Place the chopped kernels into a fine-mesh stainless-steel tea infuser with a firm latch and set aside.

Remove the peaches from the refrigerator and transfer them to an 11-quart or 12-quart copper preserving pan or a wide stainless-steel kettle. Stir well to incorporate any undissolved sugar. Taste and slowly add a little bit more of the remaining lemon juice if necessary. You should be able to taste the lemon juice, but it should not be overpowering. Add the mesh tea infuser and press down on it to submerge it.

Bring the peaches to a boil over high heat, stirring frequently with a large heatproof rubber spatula. Boil, stirring frequently, for 5 minutes. Remove from the heat and, using a large stainless-steel spoon, skim the stiff foam from the top of the mixture and discard. Mash half of the fruit with a

Continued

47

potato masher to encourage it to break down. Return the jam to the stove over medium-high heat. Cook until the jam has thickened and become cohesive, 25 to 40 minutes, decreasing the heat slightly if the mixture starts sticking.

When the jam seems ready, test it for doneness. To test, carefully transfer a representative half-spoonful of jam to one of your frozen spoons. Replace the spoon in the freezer for 3 to 4 minutes, then remove and carefully feel the underside of the spoon. It should be neither warm nor cold; if still warm, return it to the freezer for a moment. Tilt the spoon vertically to see how quickly the jam runs; if it runs very slowly, and if it has thickened to a gloppy consistency, it is done. If it runs very quickly or appears watery, cook it for another few minutes, stirring, and test again as needed. While you are waiting for the jam in the freezer to cool, skim off any white foam that appears on the surface of the jam in the pan.

When the cooking is completed, remove the mesh tea infuser. Place the peach leaf sprigs into the mixture and let steep for a few minutes off the heat. Carefully taste the jam and either remove the sprigs or leave them in for another minute or two, keeping in mind that their flavor will be slightly weaker once the jam has cooled. Using tongs, discard the peach leaf sprigs. Pour the jam into sterilized jars and process according to the manufacturer's instructions or as directed on page xiv.

Note: To peel peaches, drop them into lightly simmering water for 1 to 2 minutes, then drain them and let them rest until they are cool enough to handle. Carefully slip off the skins and proceed with the recipe.

CONCORD GRAPE JAM

Approximate Yield: five or six 8-ounce jars *Shelf Life:* 1 year

Concord grape skins paired with the subtlest hint of orange and lemon make a wow of a jam. Its flavor is intensely grapy, and its bright purple color is entrancing. Unlike familiar store-bought grape jelly, this jam is bursting with fruit, and it has just enough sugar to balance its flavor.

4 pounds stemmed Concord grapes

2 pounds white cane sugar

½ to ¾ cup strained freshly squeezed lemon juice

Very finely grated zest of ½ orange (orange part only)

½ ounce strained freshly squeezed orange juice

Scant ⅛ teaspoon citric acid

Scant ⅛ teaspoon ascorbic acid

Place a saucer with 5 metal teaspoons in a flat place in your freezer for testing the jam later.

Working directly over a small nonreactive saucepan, use your fingers to gently squeeze the flesh from each grape, being careful to catch all the grape juices in the pan. Set the skins aside in a large mixing bowl.

Over medium heat, bring the grape innards and juices to a simmer, cover, and cook until soft, 3 to 5 minutes. Immediately force as much of the pulp as possible through a fine-mesh strainer or chinois. Discard the seeds.

Continued

Add the sieved grape pulp, sugar, ½ cup of the lemon juice, the orange zest, orange juice, and citric and ascorbic acids to the grape skins, stirring well. Dip a small spoon into the liquidy part of the mixture and taste for lemon juice. If you do not detect any lemon, cautiously add a little more juice, stirring and tasting as you go, until you can just taste the tartness and lemon flavor of the juice in the mixture. Once you have reached this point, the mixture is ready to cook.

Transfer the mixture to an 11-quart or 12-quart copper preserving pan or a wide nonreactive kettle. Bring to a boil over high heat. Continue to cook until done, 20 to 30 minutes. Stir very frequently during the cooking with a heatproof rubber spatula; if the jam starts sticking, lower the heat slightly. To avoid overcooking the jam, test it for doneness after 20 minutes of cooking. When the jam is done, it will acquire a glossier sheen and will have a thicker, more luxurious look than it did initially.

To test, remove the jam from the heat and carefully transfer a representative half-spoonful to one of your frozen spoons. Replace the cold spoon in the freezer for 3 to 4 minutes, then remove and carefully feel the underside of the spoon. It should be neither warm nor cold; if still warm, return it to the freezer for a moment. Tilt the spoon vertically to see how quickly the jam runs; if it is reluctant to run, and if it has thickened to a spreadable consistency, it is done. If it runs quickly, cook it for another minute or two, stirring, and test again as needed.

When the jam is ready, skim any white foam from its surface with a stainless-steel spoon. Pour the jam into sterilized jars and process according to the manufacturer's instructions or as directed on page xiv.

TOMATO JAM

Approximate Yield: eleven or twelve 8-ounce jars *Shelf Life:* 1 year

This jam reminds us that tomatoes are a fruit, and one of the very best. Early Girl tomatoes, especially when dry farmed, work best for this jam because they are spectacularly sweet and thick-skinned. Mace and salt bring out their flavor perfectly.

9 pounds sweet tomatoes, such as Early Girl

3 pounds 15 ounces white cane sugar

⅓ to ¾ cup strained freshly squeezed lemon juice

1 small blade of mace

2 small pinches of kosher salt

Place a saucer with 5 metal teaspoons in a flat place in your freezer for testing the jam later.

Bring a medium kettle of water to a boil, then carefully drop the tomatoes into the water to loosen their skins. Leave the tomatoes immersed for 1 minute, then drain them in a large colander. When they are cool enough to handle, peel them over a large heatproof mixing bowl, discarding the skins. Place a

cutting board on a rimmed baking sheet and chop the tomatoes into medium pieces. Transfer the tomatoes and their juices back to the mixing bowl. Add the sugar and ⅓ cup of the lemon juice, stirring well to combine. Dip a small spoon into the liquidy part of the mixture and taste for lemon juice. If you do not detect any lemon, cautiously add a little more juice, stirring and tasting as you go, until you can just taste the tartness and lemon flavor of the juice

Continued

in the mixture. Once you have reached this point, the mixture is ready to cook.

Transfer the mixture to an 11-quart or 12-quart copper preserving pan or a wide nonreactive kettle. Place the mace into a fine-mesh stainless-steel tea infuser with a firm latch and add it to the mixture.

Bring the jam mixture to a boil over high heat. Add the salt and decrease the heat slightly. Skim off any surface foam with a large stainless-steel spoon. Continue to cook, monitoring the heat closely, until the jam thickens and no longer seems watery, 30 to 45 minutes. Scrape the bottom of the pan often with a heatproof rubber spatula, and decrease the heat gradually as more and more moisture cooks out of the jam. For the final 15 to 20 minutes of cooking, or when the jam starts to visibly thicken, stir the jam gently and constantly to prevent burning.

To test the jam for doneness, carefully transfer a representative half-spoonful to one of your frozen spoons. Replace the spoon in the freezer for 3 to 4 minutes, then remove and carefully feel the under-side of the spoon. It should be neither warm nor cold; if still warm, return it to the freezer for a moment. Nudge the jam gently with your finger; if it seems thick-ened and gloppy when you nudge it, it is either done or nearly done. Tilt the spoon vertically to see how quickly the jam runs; if it runs very slowly, and if it has thickened to a cohesive consistency, it is done. If it runs very quickly or appears watery, cook it for another few minutes, stirring, and test again as needed.

When the jam is ready, remove the mesh tea infuser. Skim any remaining foam from the surface of the jam. Pour the jam into sterilized jars and process according to the manufacturer's instructions or as directed on page xiv.

PEAR JAM

Approximate Yield: ten or eleven 8-ounce jars   *Shelf Life:* 8 to 10 months

Though not as acidic or bright as berries or plums, pears are surprisingly intense, and they rank among the best fruits for jam and marmalade. They are famously good for dessert; pear jam with crêpes and a light drizzle of chocolate makes a uniquely satisfying autumn treat. One thing is important above all when making anything with pear: Use the ripest, most flavorful pears you can find. A grainy-textured variety, such as Warren or Bartlett, works best.

8 pounds 2 ounces peeled and cored very ripe pears,
such as Warren or Bartlett

3 pounds 14 ounces white cane sugar

1¾ cups strained freshly squeezed lemon juice

Scant ⅛ teaspoon citric acid

Scant ⅛ teaspoon ascorbic acid

DAY 1

Chop the pears into pieces ¼ inch to ½ inch in diameter. Combine the pears, sugar, lemon juice, and citric and ascorbic acids in a hard plastic or glass storage container, stirring well to combine. Press a sheet of plastic wrap directly onto the surface of the mixture, smoothing well to minimize air bubbles (this will help keep the fruit from browning as it sits). Cover the mixture tightly with a lid and let macerate in the refrigerator overnight.

Continued

DAY 2

Place a saucer with 5 metal teaspoons in a flat place in your freezer for testing the jam later.

Remove the pears from the refrigerator and transfer them to an 11-quart or 12-quart copper preserving pan or a wide nonreactive kettle, stirring well. Position a food mill over the storage container that held the pears and set aside.

Bring the pears to a boil over high heat, stirring every 2 minutes or so. Cook, stirring frequently with a heatproof rubber spatula, until the mixture starts to thicken and the pear pieces are semi-translucent, 15 to 20 minutes. Remove from the heat and transfer one-third of the mixture to the food mill. Put as much fruit as possible through the mill, then scrape any solids that will not go through back into the jam mixture. Return the puréed fruit to the jam kettle, breaking up the chunks as you go. Place the jam over medium-high heat and continue to cook, stirring gently and constantly, until the jam has thickened and no longer appears watery, about 15 minutes more.

When the jam seems ready, test it for doneness. To test, carefully transfer a representative half-spoonful of jam to one of your frozen spoons. Replace the spoon in the freezer for 3 to 4 minutes, then remove and carefully feel the underside of the spoon. It should be neither warm nor cold; if still warm, return it to the freezer for a moment. Tilt the spoon vertically to see how quickly the jam runs; if it runs slowly, and if it has thickened to a gloppy consistency, it is done. If it runs very quickly or appears watery, cook it for another few minutes, stirring, and test again as needed. While you are waiting for the jam in the freezer to cool, skim off any white foam that appears on the surface of the jam in the pan. Pour the jam into sterilized jars and process according to the manufacturer's instructions or as directed on page xiv.

Variations:

PEAR JAM WITH ROSEMARY & PINE

Cook the jam as directed. When the cooking is completed, place two or three 6-inch sprigs rosemary into the jam and let steep for a few minutes off the heat. Stir and carefully taste the jam and either remove the sprigs or leave them for another minute or two, keeping in mind that their flavor will be slightly weaker once the jam has cooled. Using tongs, discard the rosemary. Add a generous drizzle of pinecone bud syrup and stir well. Process as directed.

PEAR JAM WITH VANILLA & ELDERFLOWER

To make this delicately flavored jam, cook the jam as directed, adding one 2-inch to 3-inch piece vanilla bean, split and scraped, to the mixture at the start of cooking. Just moments before the jam is finished cooking, stir in a generous splash of elderflower liqueur. Cook for a minute or two more to allow some of the alcohol to evaporate, then remove the vanilla bean. Process as directed.

PEAR JAM WITH CHESTNUT HONEY & SAGE

Cook the jam as directed. When the cooking is completed, stir in 1 to 2 ounces chestnut honey and several drops of chestnut honey vinegar or apple cider vinegar to taste; its flavor should be mild. Place a small bunch of fresh sage into the mixture and let steep for 1 to 2 minutes off the heat. Stir and carefully taste the jam and either remove the sage or leave it in for another minute or two; its flavor should be subtle, but keep in mind that it will mellow slightly as the jam cools. Using tongs, discard the sage. Process as directed.

QUINCE-APPLE BUTTER

Approximate Yield: eight 8-ounce jars *Shelf Life:* 2 years

Quince and apple make a lovely butter with a very perfumy autumnal flavor. Adding a little elderflower liqueur to the butter brings out the floral notes of the quince. Use a very tart apple for this butter for best results.

3¼ pounds firm, crisp apples (preferably pink-fleshed or tart red-skinned),
cut into eighths

1¾ pounds quinces, cut into eighths

2½ pounds white cane sugar

⅓ to ⅔ cup strained freshly squeezed lemon juice

Scant ⅛ teaspoon citric acid

Scant ⅛ teaspoon ascorbic acid

Several drops of elderflower liqueur (optional)

Place the apples and quinces in a large nonreactive pot. Add enough cold water to just cover the fruit. Bring the mixture to a boil over medium-high heat, adjust the heat to medium-low, cover, and cook until the fruit is extremely soft and the quinces have turned rosy, about 3 hours. Stir the fruit periodically as it cooks, lowering the heat and/or adding a little more water if the mixture starts to stick.

Put the fruit and its liquid through the finest disc of a food mill into a large bowl, forcing through as much purée as possible before discarding the remaining solids.

Place a saucer with 5 metal teaspoons in a flat place in your freezer for testing the butter later.

Add the sugar to the fruit purée along with ⅓ cup of the lemon juice and the citric and ascorbic acids. Dip a small spoon into the mixture and taste. If you do not detect any lemon, cautiously add a little bit more juice, stirring and tasting as you go, until you can just taste the tartness and lemon flavor of the juice in the mixture. Once you have reached this point, the mixture is ready to cook.

Transfer the mixture to an 11-quart or 12-quart copper preserving pan or a wide nonreactive kettle. Bring the mixture to a boil over high heat, stirring frequently to prevent sticking, and cook, monitoring the heat closely, until the butter thickens, 20 to 40 minutes. The mixture will spit and splatter; wear an oven mitt and long sleeves and stand as far back as possible, scraping the bottom of the pan often with a heatproof rubber spatula. Decrease the heat slightly as more and more moisture cooks out of the butter, stirring slowly and constantly to avoid sticking.

When the butter has thickened and darkened and appears slightly shiny, test the butter for doneness. To test, remove the butter from the heat and carefully transfer a half-spoonful of butter to one of your frozen spoons. Place the spoon back in the freezer for 3 to 4 minutes, then remove and carefully feel the underside of the spoon. It should be neither warm nor cold; if still warm, return it to the freezer for a moment. Tilt the spoon vertically to see how quickly the butter runs; if it does not run, and if its top layer has thickened to a paste-like consistency, it is done. If it runs or appears liquidy, cook it for another few minutes, stirring, and test again as needed.

Stir in the elderflower liqueur, if using. Pour the butter into sterilized jars and process according to the manufacturer's instructions or as directed on page xiv.

Variation:
QUINCE-PEAR BUTTER
Replace the apples with pears. Omit the elderflower liqueur. At the start of the final cooking, add a small pinch of ground allspice and a large pinch of kosher salt to the mixture. Proceed with the rest of the recipe as directed.

FRUITED IRISH BROWN BREAD

Yield: one 6½-inch round loaf

Brown breads are standard everyday fare in Ireland, where they are eaten at all times of day. For this version, I have incorporated a flavorful mix of spices and marmalade into the dough itself. Toasted and slathered with some salty butter and honey, this bread makes one beautiful breakfast.

½ cup whole milk

½ teaspoon apple cider vinegar

1½ cups unbleached all-purpose flour, plus more for dusting

1 cup Irish wholemeal flour or stone-ground whole-wheat flour

½ cup oat flour

¼ cup sugar, plus more for sprinkling

2 teaspoons baking soda

1 teaspoon kosher salt

1 teaspoon ground ginger

1 teaspoon apple pie spice

1½ teaspoons caraway seeds

¾ cup English Marmalade (page 7), coarsely chopped if thick-cut

1 large egg

5 tablespoons cold unsalted butter (preferably European-style)

½ cup dark raisins

¼ cup golden raisins

¾ cup coarsely chopped walnuts

¼ cup heavy cream

Position a rack in the middle of the oven and preheat the oven to 400°F. Line a small baking sheet with parchment paper and set aside.

In a glass measuring cup, combine the milk with the vinegar and let sit for a few minutes to sour the milk.

In a large bowl, whisk together the all-purpose flour, wholemeal flour, oat flour, sugar, baking soda, salt, ginger, apple pie spice, and caraway seeds. Add the marmalade and egg to the soured milk, whisk to combine, and set aside.

Cut the butter into small cubes and sprinkle them over the flour mixture. Using your fingers, rub the butter quickly into the flour mixture until no large pieces remain. Whisk in the raisins and walnuts and make a well in the center.

Pour the marmalade mixture into the well all at once. Using a strong, wide, long-handled butter knife, stir quickly from the

Continued

center of the bowl, gradually drawing in the dry ingredients from the periphery, just until the dough comes together and no dry flour remains.

Turn the dough out onto a lightly floured board. Pat and shape the dough into a 6½-inch round. Flip the dough over and continue shaping it into a perfect 6½-inch round loaf that is 1½ inches thick. Transfer it to the prepared baking sheet. Using a sharp knife, cut a deep cross in the top of the loaf. Brush the loaf liberally with the cream and sprinkle with a little sugar.

Bake the loaf for 10 minutes, then lower the heat to 350°F and continue baking until the loaf is golden brown and a tester inserted in the center comes out clean, about another 45 minutes. Let cool on a rack for at least 30 minutes before slicing.

BRUSSELS SPROUTS WITH KUMQUATS & SMOKED SALT

Yield: Serves 4

This extraordinary juxtaposition of flavors and textures is an irresistible crowd-pleaser. Browned brussels sprouts, just starting to fall apart, plus chewy candied kumquats and smoked salt, all set against a rich background of bacon: Need I say more?

¼ cup bacon fat

1 pound brussels sprouts, sliced lengthwise into thirds

5 tablespoons Kumquat Marmalade (page 15)

2 large pinches of smoked sea salt

Melt the bacon fat in a shallow 12-inch enameled cast-iron pan over low heat. Add the brussels sprouts, toss well, and cover. Allow the sprouts to cook without stirring for 5 to 6 minutes, and then toss well. Re-cover and continue cooking the sprouts, tossing every few minutes, until the sprouts are tender and browned, another 8 to 9 minutes. Immediately remove from the heat and add the marmalade and salt. Toss well, taste for seasoning, and serve at once.

BEET SOUP WITH PLUMS & CORIANDER YOGURT

Yield: Serves 8

This exquisitely balanced soup boasts a striking combination of colors and flavors. It is an unusual and ingenious use for plum jam, whose hue and tartness perfectly enhance the beets. The bright garlicky coriander yogurt and parsley garnishes show off the beauty of the soup brilliantly.

SOUP

¼ cup neutral-flavored olive oil

1 medium yellow onion, thinly sliced

4 cloves garlic, finely chopped

2 ribs celery, thinly sliced

¼ teaspoon cayenne pepper

¼ teaspoon sweet paprika

Freshly ground black pepper

2½ pounds dark red beets, peeled and cut into ½-inch cubes

½ pound russet potatoes, peeled and cut into ½-inch cubes

½ cup Plum Jam (page 34), made with red or purple plums

Freshly squeezed lime juice, as needed

Kosher salt

1½ cups whole-milk yogurt (not Greek)

2 cloves garlic, very finely grated

½ teaspoon kosher salt

2 teaspoons coriander seeds

½ cup finely chopped fresh flat-leaf parsley

To make the soup, heat the olive oil in an 8-quart soup pot over medium heat. Add the onion, garlic, and celery and sauté until wilted and verging on translucent, about 5 minutes. Sprinkle the cayenne, paprika, and several grinds of black pepper over the onion mixture and continue cooking for another 1 to 2 minutes.

Add the beets, potatoes, plum jam, and 9 cups water. Bring the mixture to a boil over high heat, then lower the heat and simmer gently for 1 hour, or until the beets and potatoes are very tender. Purée the soup using a handheld immersion blender. Add a few squeezes of lime juice and salt to taste.

To make the coriander yogurt, while the soup simmers, place the yogurt in a bowl and add the garlic and salt. Toast the coriander seeds briefly by placing them in a small cast-iron skillet and shaking them over medium heat until they release their aroma. Transfer the seeds to a mortar and grind them finely. Add the ground coriander seeds to the yogurt mixture and stir very well with a fork to combine. Cover well and chill until needed. The yogurt is best within 1 hour of being made.

To serve the soup, ladle it into warm bowls. Drizzle each serving with 2 to 3 tablespoons coriander yogurt and sprinkle with 1 tablespoon parsley.

BEET SOUP WITH PLUMS & CORIANDER YOGURT

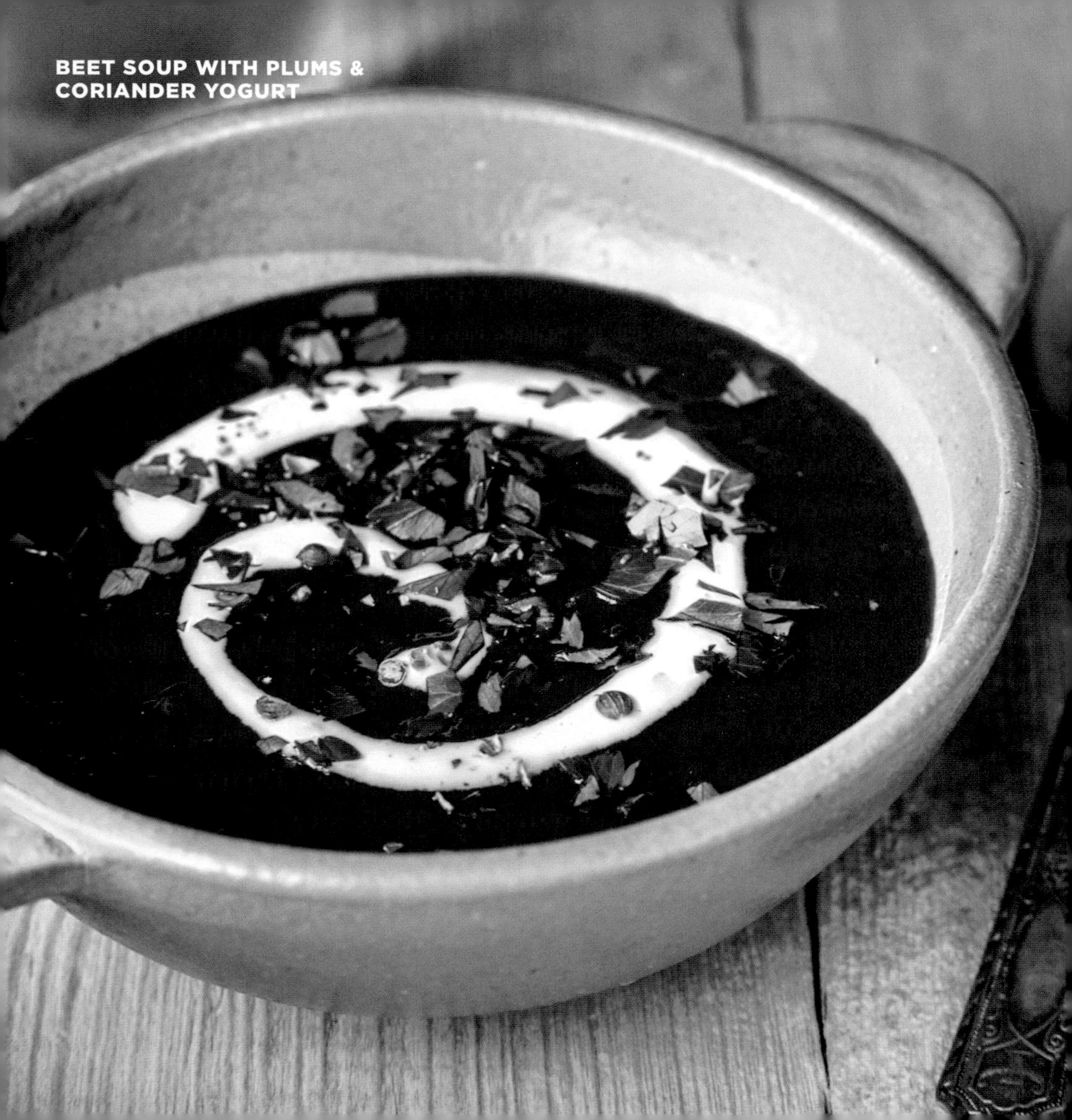

BRAISED SHORT RIBS
IN BERRIES & RED WINE

BRAISED SHORT RIBS IN BERRIES & RED WINE

Yield: Serves 3 or 4

This satisfying weekday braise features meat so tender it falls apart, bathed in the lush fruitiness of dark berry jam (try the Blackberry Jam, page 28) and red wine. My favorite way to serve this is with blue cheese–enhanced buckwheat polenta and a spunky watercress-tomato salad with balsamic vinaigrette. This dish needs to be made a day ahead of time to reach its greatest potential.

1¼ pounds beef short ribs

½ large yellow onion, very thinly sliced

½ cup dark berry jam, such as elderberry, mulberry, blackberry, or black currant

½ cup medium-bodied red wine

8 sprigs thyme

1 bay leaf

1 teaspoon juniper berries

½ teaspoon kosher salt

Freshly ground black pepper

Combine the short ribs, onion, jam, wine, thyme, bay leaf, juniper berries, salt, and several grinds of pepper in a 3-quart slow cooker. Cover, turn the heat to low, and cook for 8 hours.

Using a large slotted spoon, transfer the meat and aromatics to a bowl, draining well, and loosely cover. Transfer the liquid to a separate bowl and loosely cover. Place both bowls in the refrigerator to chill overnight.

Remove the bowls from the refrigerator. Discard the fat layer that has formed on the surface of the cooking liquids, as well as any solid pieces of fat that have appeared on and around the meat solids. Discard the bay leaf and any juniper berries and thyme sprigs you can see. Transfer the liquids to the meat, cover, and refrigerate until needed. To serve, reheat in a saucepan over low heat. This keeps well frozen in an airtight container for up to 3 months.

CHICKEN "TAGINE" WITH TURNIPS & APRICOTS

Yield: Serves 6

This recipe is a lively one-dish meal bursting with the crunch of toasted almonds, the brightness of chopped fresh herbs, the sweet-sour acidity of pickled lemons and apricot, and the earthiness of turnips and chicken. A wonderful illustration of the savory possibilities of apricot jam, this dish is ideal for a dinner party; prepare each ingredient in the afternoon and brown the chicken ahead of time and you will be free and able to enjoy a cocktail with your guests while the stew cooks.

Large handful of sliced unblanched almonds

3 chicken thighs

3 chicken drumsticks

Kosher salt and freshly ground black pepper

Crushed dried thyme (preferably Moroccan), for rubbing

1 medium yellow onion

3 cloves garlic, thickly sliced

2½ tablespoons unsalted butter (preferably European-style)

2 tablespoons neutral-flavored olive oil

¾ cup Apricot Jam (page 25)

½ teaspoon ground ginger

Small pinch of saffron threads

2 (3-inch) cinnamon sticks

10 green cardamom pods, smashed

2 bay leaves

1 pound turnips, peeled and cut into ¾-inch wedges

2 large carrots, peeled and cut into ½-inch rounds

Juice of 1 lemon (not Meyer)

2 preserved lemons (preferably Meyer), seeded and chopped

Handful of chopped fresh flat-leaf parsley

Handful of chopped fresh cilantro

First, lightly toast the almonds: Position a rack in the middle of the oven and preheat the oven to 350°F. Place the almonds in a single layer on a baking sheet and toast them until pale golden, 5 to 7 minutes. Transfer them to a plate to cool completely.

Rub the chicken pieces all over with salt, pepper, and thyme. Cut the onion into large chunks and place the onion with the garlic in a small food processor. Pulse briefly just until the onion is uniformly finely chopped, making sure to stop before it turns into a paste. Set aside.

Heat the butter and oil in a shallow heavy-bottomed 12-inch pan over medium-high heat. Add the chicken pieces and brown them on all sides. Transfer to a plate.

Continued

Lower the heat to medium. Add the onion mixture and sauté until translucent, about 10 minutes. Add the jam, ginger, saffron, cinnamon, cardamom, and bay leaves and stir well. Nestle the chicken pieces into the onion mixture, add ¼ inch water, decrease the heat to medium-low, and cover the pan. Braise the chicken for 15 minutes.

Scatter the turnips and carrots evenly over the chicken. Do not stir. Cover and braise until the vegetables and chicken are tender, about another 30 minutes.

Use tongs to transfer the chicken to a plate. Cover the chicken loosely with aluminum foil to keep warm. Add the lemon juice, preserved lemons, and half the parsley and cilantro to the sauce. Increase the heat to medium-high and simmer, stirring frequently, until the sauce has reduced to a jammy consistency. Return the chicken to the sauce to warm through, turning to coat the chicken with the sauce. Remove the pan from the heat and sprinkle the tagine with the remaining parsley and cilantro and the almonds. Generously grind black pepper over all. Serve at once.

STRAWBERRY SANGRIA

Yield: Serves 8

Recipes for sangria abound, but including strawberry jam in the mix adds viscosity and extra depth of flavor. Macerating fresh strawberries in red wine is an old Italian trick that I borrowed for this recipe, and it works wonders. To accentuate the berry flavor even more, I added a little Marsala in addition to the brandy. Fewer drinks could be more tempting on a warm July night— or better suited to a crowd.

1 orange, seeded and sliced crosswise into thin wheels

1 lemon, seeded and sliced crosswise into thin wheels

¼ cup strained freshly squeezed orange juice

Scant ¼ cup strained freshly squeezed lemon juice

1½ cups Strawberry Jam (page 21)

½ cup brandy

½ cup sweet Marsala

1 (750-ml) bottle medium-bodied red wine

2 cups fresh strawberries, thickly sliced

Place the orange and lemon slices in a large pitcher or small punch bowl. Add the orange and lemon juices and mash gently with a muddler or wooden spoon, taking care not to damage the pieces of fruit; you just want to bruise them enough for them to release their flavor. Add the jam and muddle a little more, then add the brandy, Marsala, red wine, and ½ cup water and stir very well.

Stir in the strawberries. Cover the sangria with plastic wrap and let it rest at room temperature for 2 hours. Then chill the sangria until cold.

To serve, ladle the sangria into chilled glasses, making sure to include some strawberry slices in each serving.

ALESSANDRA'S CROSTATA

Yield: one 10-inch tart *Serves:* 8 to 12

When I first visited my friend Alessandra, who lives in Turin, I arrived at her house weary with travel, to be welcomed by one of the most beautiful latticed jam-filled tarts I had ever seen. One of the highlights of that trip was the lesson Alessandra gave me in how to make crostata, her mother's recipe. I now share it with you. You can fill the tart with any favorite jam or marmalade; great options include elderberry-orange marmalade, Strawberry Jam (page 21), or a mixture of orange marmalade and Kumquat Marmalade (page 15). Choose lemon or orange zest and a liqueur to enhance your jam choice.

PASTRY DOUGH

7½ tablespoons unsalted butter (preferably European-style),
at room temperature, plus more for buttering the pan

1¾ cups Italian "00" flour or unbleached all-purpose flour, plus more for dusting

7 tablespoons plus 1 teaspoon sugar

2 teaspoons baking powder

Pinch of kosher salt

2 large eggs, separated, at room temperature

Finely grated zest of 1 lemon or most of 1 orange

FILLING

1 cup Strawberry Jam (page 21) or a jam or marmalade of your choice

Small splash of kirsch or a liqueur or liquor of your choice

to match the jam (optional)

Position a rack in the middle of the oven and preheat the oven to 350°F. Butter a 10-inch round cake pan or fluted tart pan with a removable bottom and line the bottom with parchment paper. Set aside.

To make the dough, whisk together the flour, sugar, baking powder, and salt in a medium bowl. Add the butter, egg yolks, lemon zest, and 3 tablespoons water and mix well with your hands or a fork. Add more water as needed, 1 tablespoon at a time, until the dough comes together into a moist ball. Let the dough rest for at least 10 minutes at room temperature, or wrap the dough in plastic wrap and refrigerate for up to 24 hours. Freeze for longer storage.

Turn the dough onto a well-floured work surface and sprinkle a little flour over the dough. Knead the dough briefly, sprinkling with more flour as needed, until the dough is smooth and supple. Cut off one third of the dough and reserve. Roll the remaining two-thirds of the dough into an even 12-inch circle. Fit the dough carefully into the prepared pan. Using a fluted ravioli cutter, go around the edge of the dough to trim the walls of the crust to an even ⅝-inch height. Add the dough trimmings to the reserved dough. In a small bowl, beat the egg whites with a fork to loosen them. Brush the bottom of the pastry shell with some of the egg whites.

Continued

Roll the reserved dough into a 12-inch-long oval. Using a fluted ravioli cutter, cut 14 long strips of dough, each about ⅓ inch wide. You should have exactly enough dough. Carefully separate the strips from each other and let them rest at room temperature for at least 30 minutes or as long as 2 hours.

To make the filling, in a small bowl, stir the jam with a fork. Add the kirsch and stir to thin the jam slightly. Spread the jam evenly in the prepared tart shell, taking care that any chunks of fruit are evenly distributed. Position the dough strips over the jam in a perpendicular lattice, starting in the middle of the tart and using 7 strips of dough for each direction. Run your ravioli cutter around the perimeter of the tart to trim the excess dough, help the lattice strips adhere to the bottom crust, and create an even height approximately ⅛ inch above the surface of the jam. Discard the dough scraps. Brush the lattice with the remaining egg whites.

Bake the crostata until golden, 35 to 40 minutes. Then, if you prefer it dry as the Italians do, leave it in the turned-off oven with the door wide open to dry out for 30 minutes or so before transferring it to a cooling rack. Otherwise, simply place the crostata in its pan on a rack to cool. When the crostata has cooled completely, invert it onto a plate, peel off the parchment, and turn right side up to serve.

BLACK SESAME–FIG ICE CREAM

Yield: 1 quart

This exotic ice cream has a rich, savory character all its own. Black sesame has a strong, nutty flavor, and the ice cream is speckled with fig seeds and pieces of candied fig. The texture is very creamy and just sweet enough for the flavors to shine. Serve this with a trickle of honey or chocolate over the top and a very crisp nutty cookie alongside.

⅔ cup black sesame seeds

2 cups heavy cream

½ cup whole milk

2 vanilla beans, split lengthwise

4 large egg yolks

¼ cup sugar

4 pinches of kosher salt

1 cup Black Mission Fig Jam (page 32)

Toast the sesame seeds briefly in a large skillet over medium heat, tossing them until they start to pop. Immediately transfer them to a plate to cool, then to a food processor fitted with a metal blade. Grind the sesame seeds, making sure to stop short of turning them into a paste.

In a medium saucepan, heat the cream and milk to just under scalding. Stir in the ground sesame seeds. Scrape the seeds from the vanilla beans into the cream mixture and also drop in the pods. Cover and let steep for 30 minutes. Pour the milk mixture through a fine-mesh sieve into a bowl, pressing on the solids to obtain every last drop of flavor. Discard the solids.

In a medium saucepan, whisk the egg yolks with the sugar and salt until smooth. Gradually whisk in the warm milk mixture. Place the saucepan over low heat. Using a heatproof rubber spatula, stir the custard constantly and quickly until it starts to thicken. Immediately remove the pan from the heat and continue stirring the custard off the heat for 1 minute to cool it and prevent it from curdling. Place the custard on a rack to cool. Press plastic wrap directly onto the surface of the custard and refrigerate for at least 4 hours or overnight. Meanwhile, put a medium storage container or bowl in the freezer to chill.

Freeze the ice cream in an ice-cream machine according to the manufacturer's instructions. Have the fig jam close at hand. As soon as the ice cream starts to look slushy, with the machine running, add the fig jam a little bit at a time. Continue churning just until the ice cream has thickened but is not completely firm. Immediately transfer it to the frozen bowl. Working very quickly so the ice cream does not start to melt, press plastic wrap directly onto the surface of the ice cream. Place the ice cream in the freezer to chill overnight before serving.

METRIC CONVERSIONS & EQUIVALENTS

METRIC CONVERSION FORMULAS

To Convert	Multiply
Ounces to grams	Ounces by 28.35
Pounds to kilograms	Pounds by .454
Teaspoons to milliliters	Teaspoons by 4.93
Tablespoons to milliliters	Tablespoons by 14.79
Fluid ounces to milliliters	Fluid ounces by 29.57
Cups to milliliters	Cups by 236.59
Cups to liters	Cups by .236
Pints to liters	Pints by .473
Quarts to liters	Quarts by .946
Gallons to liters	Gallons by 3.785
Inches to centimeters	Inches by 2.54

COMMON INGREDIENTS AND THEIR APPROXIMATE EQUIVALENTS

1 cup all-purpose flour = 140 grams

1 stick butter (4 ounces • ½ cup • 8 tablespoons) = 110 grams

1 cup butter (8 ounces • 2 sticks • 16 tablespoons) = 220 grams

1 cup brown sugar, firmly packed = 225 grams

1 cup granulated sugar = 200 grams

OVEN TEMPERATURES

To convert Fahrenheit to Celsius, subtract 32 from Fahrenheit, multiply the result by 5, then divide by 9.

Description	Fahrenheit	Celsius	British Gas Mark
Very cool	200°	95°	0
Very cool	225°	110°	¼
Very cool	250°	120°	½
Cool	275°	135°	1
Cool	300°	150°	2
Warm	325°	165°	3
Moderate	350°	175°	4
Moderately hot	375°	190°	5
Fairly hot	400°	200°	6
Hot	425°	220°	7
Very hot	450°	230°	8
Very hot	475°	245°	9

Information compiled from a variety of sources, including *Recipes into Type* by Joan Whitman and Dolores Simon (Newton, MA: Biscuit Books, 1993); *The New Food Lover's Companion* by Sharon Tyler Herbst (Hauppauge, NY: Barron's, 2013); and *Rosemary Brown's Big Kitchen Instruction Book* (Kansas City, MO: Andrews McMeel, 1998).

APPROXIMATE METRIC EQUIVALENTS

Volume

¼ teaspoon	1 milliliter
½ teaspoon	2.5 milliliters
¾ teaspoon	4 milliliters
1 teaspoon	5 milliliters
1¼ teaspoons	6 milliliters
1½ teaspoons	7.5 milliliters
1¾ teaspoons	8.5 milliliters
2 teaspoons	10 milliliters
1 tablespoon (½ fluid ounce)	15 milliliters
2 tablespoons (1 fluid ounce)	30 milliliters
¼ cup	60 milliliters
⅓ cup	80 milliliters
½ cup (4 fluid ounces)	120 milliliters
⅔ cup	160 milliliters
¾ cup	180 milliliters
1 cup (8 fluid ounces)	240 milliliters
1¼ cups	300 milliliters
1½ cups (12 fluid ounces)	360 milliliters
1⅔ cups	400 milliliters
2 cups (1 pint)	460 milliliters
3 cups	700 milliliters
4 cups (1 quart)	.95 liter
1 quart plus ¼ cup	1 liter
4 quarts (1 gallon)	3.8 liters

Weight

¼ ounce	7 grams
½ ounce	14 grams
¾ ounce	21 grams
1 ounce	28 grams
1¼ ounces	35 grams
1½ ounces	42.5 grams
1⅔ ounces	45 grams
2 ounces	57 grams
3 ounces	85 grams
4 ounces (¼ pound)	113 grams
5 ounces	142 grams
6 ounces	170 grams
7 ounces	198 grams
8 ounces (½ pound)	227 grams
16 ounces (1 pound)	454 grams
35.25 ounces (2.2 pounds)	1 kilogram

Length

⅛ inch	3 millimeters
¼ inch	6 millimeters
½ inch	1¼ centimeters
1 inch	2½ centimeters
2 inches	5 centimeters
2½ inches	6 centimeters
4 inches	10 centimeters
5 inches	13 centimeters
6 inches	15¼ centimeters
12 inches (1 foot)	30 centimeters

INDEX

Andrews McMeel Publishing
a division of Andrews McMeel Universal
1130 Walnut Street, Kansas City, Missouri 64106

www.andrewsmcmeel.com
www.bluechairfruit.com

17 18 19 20 21 SDB 10 9 8 7 6 5 4 3 2 1

ISBN: 978-1-4494-8040-0

Library of Congress Control Number: 2016951172

Editor: Jean Z. Lucas
Art Director: Julie Barnes
Photographer: Sara Remington
Production Editor: Maureen Sullivan
Production Manager: Carol Coe

ATTENTION: SCHOOLS AND BUSINESSES
Andrews McMeel books are available at quantity discounts with
bulk purchase for educational, business, or sales promotional use.
For information, please e-mail the Andrews McMeel Publishing
Special Sales Department: specialsales@amuniversal.com.